ATTAINMENT
THE 12 ELEMENTS OF ELITE PERFORMANCE

TROY BASSHAM

All rights reserved. No part of this book may be reproduced or transmitted in any form or by means now known or any means yet to be invented, electronic, or mechanical, including photocopying, recording, or by any information storage or retrieval system without written permission for the author or publisher, except brief inclusion of quotations in a review.

Copyright © 2012 by Mental Management® Systems LLC
and Troy Bassham. All rights reserved.

The term Mental Management® is registered
and owned by Lanny Bassham.

All rights reserved.
ISBN 978-1-934324-27-1

Printed in the United States of America

Order from
Mental Management® Systems
www.mentalmanagement.com
ph. 972-899-9640

CONTENTS

INTRODUCTION	1
CHAPTER 1 - PASSION	5
CHAPTER 2 - OPPORTUNITY	21
CHAPTER 3 - TRAINING WITH PURPOSE	35
CHAPTER 4 - BECOME MENTALLY STRONG	51
CHAPTER 5 - SELF-IMAGE OF A WINNER	75
THE 12 ELEMENTS	93

DEDICATION

To my wife Frances, my reason for reaching success.

ACKNOWLEDGEMENTS

To Christ who gives me strength and makes all things possible.

To my daughters Tori and Sydney for making me feel like a winner each and every day.

To my parents, Lanny and Helen who started me in my journey.

To my brother Brian for the support and competition growing up.

To my sister Heather for the encouragement you give.

The University of Texas at El Paso, and the United States Army Marksmanship Unit for the opportunity.

To Patrick Combs for the challenge you presented.

To all my students who strive to be the best.

INTRODUCTION

I grew up having the privilege of knowing some of the best athletes in the world in their respected sports. I didn't just meet Olympic and World Champions, I knew many of these people and learned a lot from them over the years.

I can tell you that the best of the best in sport, business, education, and life, all have one thing in common. They all think differently from the average person. They follow a different set of guidelines and these guidelines, or elements as I refer to them, are what gives them an advantage over their competition.

In life we are competing in many different areas. How well we handle these areas will provide us with an advantage or give us a disadvantage in terms of being successful. This book breaks down the twelve elements that separate the elite competitor from the average competitor. My goal is to give you an advantage and share with you how I used these elements to reach important goals. I also share stories from a variety of elite performers to inspire and influence you in a way that will improve your chances of reaching your goals in becoming the best you can be.

Whether you're an athlete, business professional, salesperson, coach, or educator, success doesn't happen by accident. It takes careful planning, time, energy and effort to reach top levels in any profession. Most individuals have a good grasp on planning and building the necessary skills along with the subconscious ability it takes to perform tasks proficiently.

What separates the elite performers from the next tier of professionals isn't planning, and in most cases it isn't the amount of effort or energy that is given. It's not the ability to do the job at hand, nor the amount of equipment available. You need all the above, along with experience in order to be good. But to reach the top level of success it takes something else, something that can only come from within.

Your willingness to change the Self-Image you have and replace it with the Self-Image you need is crucial in order to truly succeed at the highest level. Let's take a close look at what separates the good from the great, I'll break it down into five parts:

Passion
Opportunity
Purposeful Practice
A Strong Mental Game
The Self-Image of a Winner

All five of these areas are found in elite performers. Without these necessary five components it's difficult to reach your top level of achievement. As we move forward you will notice that the elements of elite performers are found in each of these parts.

CHAPTER 1 - PASSION

Great athletes, musicians, business professionals and coaches all have the passion and drive to do what they do. The passion for the process is the willingness to do something without outside external motivation from others. Tiger Woods did not become the best golfer in the world by having his dad, Earl Woods, tell him it was time to practice. There are countless stories of Earl Woods telling Tiger it's time to quit practicing because it's getting late.

Michael Jordan never had to be reminded when he needed to practice basketball. He made it a habit to be the first one at practice and the last one to leave. It was the love of the game and the drive to get better that helped make him become the greatest basketball player of all time.

Eric Clapton didn't need to have someone force him to play the guitar. He spent countless hours practicing because he would rather learn how to play the guitar than do anything else. His passion for playing guitar was so great that it got him expelled from Kingston College of Art for

ELEMENT #1

Elite Performers are passionate about what they do. Others like what they do.

playing his guitar during class. The result of his passion vaulted him into becoming one of the greatest guitarists of all time.

Even in the business world we can see the same passion and drive that separates the average competitor from the elite. Steve Jobs, late CEO of Apple Computers, had a passion for innovation that has changed the way we live today. When Jobs co-founded Apple, he changed personal computing with the Mac. He was able to bring Apple to the forefront of the music and digital world in 2003 when he introduced the iPod and iTunes. Being the Co-founder of Apple was just the beginning of showing the world his passion for innovation. Jobs was also responsible for bringing Pixar Inc. to the forefront of the animation world. Pixar has changed the way animation films are produced.

Elite Performers are passionate about what they do. Others like what they do.

You either have the passion or you don't. It's not something that an outside source can generate. We may be able to help guide someone into finding their passion, but it's not something that a coach or mentor can provide. At best, all a coach, mentor, teacher, or manager can do is to help pull out the drive that is already inside the individual. If one does not have the passion, he will struggle to become successful at his task. To really reach the area of being elite, you have to be passionate about the job you are doing.

When the going gets tough

When the going gets tough, the ones with passion drive through. Individuals who are passionate about what they do view the tough situations as necessary learning experiences in order for them to grow. A non-passionate individual views the tough situations as excuses and reasons as to why he or she cannot succeed.

During the 1960s and 1970s, my father was the best of the best. He had won at every level, from Junior National Champion to the Olympic Gold Medal in 1976. He held national records and had world titles that others would only hope to achieve. Like many sons growing up, I wanted to follow in my dad's footsteps.

My father didn't allow my twin brother, Brian, and me to start shooting until we were fourteen. I remember begging him to let us shoot for years and being turned down over and over. On the first day I finally had the chance to shoot, I was hooked. I knew I wanted to be a rifle shooter. I wanted to be a winner like the shooters that surrounded me growing up. I wanted to win the National Championships and represent my country in the sport of rifle shooting.

I realized that my passion was to challenge myself to win at every level of shooting. I wanted to win at the junior level, the college level, the national level and the international level. I wanted to wear the red, white and blue and represent my country in the sport I loved. I enjoyed shooting and was particularly good at the conventional style of rifle shooting over the international style. I enjoyed the challenge of trying to master a sport where you had to make the body stop and hit a target that could be as small as 0.5 millimeters in diameter; the size of the tip of a pencil.

I found myself going to the shooting range after school to practice while my friends did other things. I felt an inner pull to train and improve. It wasn't a matter of how much shooting I did, but rather the desire to just go and shoot. The range became a place of accomplishment for me.

The first competition that my brother and I competed in was the Texas State Rifle Championships. You would think that a smaller competition would be a good place to get your feet wet, but not for us. Texas is a gun friendly state and there are many great shooters who compete for the state title. This competition was also a qualifier for the National Championships. Our nerves were tested, but we took first and second in our division. I won my first competition and followed it up by winning the National Championships in the junior division eight months later.

During my first three years of shooting I would win two national titles and make my first World Championship team. I would fare better than my brother, and looking back, I realize it was not talent or ability that separated us during this period in our shooting career. I believe it had more to do with my passion for shooting over his. I found myself practicing at the range by myself on several occasions. I also stopped playing high school soccer while my brother continued to play all four years. He simply didn't have the same drive for shooting as I did.

If you do not strive to push yourself while others do, what chance do you have of winning? I work with a lot of junior golfers who aspire to be on the PGA Tour someday. It's amazing how many of them want to play professionally but don't have the passion for the sport. They all like to play, but many of them do not have the drive and passion to go out and train like they should.

When you see a young high school student at seventeen years of age who would rather go to the golf course and work on his game than go to the movies with some friends on a Friday afternoon, you have to ask yourself why? Most teenagers would choose to go out with their friends, especially after practicing hard throughout the week. Passion is the only answer. I am not saying they cannot go out and have fun; what I am saying is that these individuals prioritize their schedules based on their passion.

Passion is the first part of becoming the best you can be. If you question whether you have the passion, you need to ask yourself, what is my participation level? There are three participation levels.

What is your participation level?

- Training to Learn
- Training to Compete
- Training to Win

This is a question I ask all of my clients. If you don't know what your participation level is, how can you set goals and properly develop the right training schedule? Your desire dictates your participation level.

Participation Level #1: Training to Learn

We all start off in this participation level. To become successful we must first learn. At the beginning stage it's about learning and mastering the basics of the sport or activity we have chosen. In shooting, you cannot shoot a good score until you learn the proper way to hold the rifle and get a consistent position. In golf you cannot score until you learn how to swing the club and read putts. In sales you cannot go out and sell a product or service until you know about the product and service you are providing, nor can you go out and make the sales you need without the proper basic skills of selling. We all have to start from the beginning and therefore we are all automatically in the learning participation level.

If you are in the Training to Learn Level it does not mean that you will not have some success. This level may be the starting point, but there are many individuals who can become good in this level. We see this in Clay Shooting and Dog Agility. In these two examples many of the competitors are successful business people who are juggling their life, their career, and their sport at the same time. Training is not something they can do every day, so they may have to settle for a two or three times a week format. With the right equipment and proper instruction one can get good enough to learn the sport or activity within this short amount of time. These individuals are able to take their success in business and incorporate it into their new activity.

We also see successful athletes excel in business because they have already gone through this learning level previously. Building a base in anything starts with mastering the basics. It's in the Training to Learn Level that the mastering of basics is so important. If you don't master the basics in this level and move onto the next participation level you will slow down your progress and development.

Participation Level #2: Training to Compete

There comes a time when going to competitions or just showing up for work doesn't cut it anymore. When a person finds himself wanting to strive at a higher level and advance in his career, he must move out of the Training to Learn Level and enter the Training to Compete Level.

Training to Compete means you must raise your level of training and commitment. It means setting goals to see progress and challenging yourself to reach the next level. This participation level isn't one that is going to automatically make you a winner, but it does improve the likelihood that you can win and achieve your goals.

Depending on how you define winning will determine if you win at this participation level. I define winning as when a person achieves or reaches levels beyond his past performances. For example, a golfer who has never shot a score below par in a tournament wins when he or she accomplishes shooting under par in a tournament. A team that has never made the playoffs wins when they make the playoffs. A person who makes the Olympic team for the first time is a winner. It's not always about finishing in first place that defines a winner. Winning is all about continuous improvements of the individual's process, not necessarily the direct outcome. It is important to remember that improving the process is what defines success. Defining winning in this way makes it possible for the person at this level to move forward in his or her progression. This is a must for those who strive to be the best they can be.

People compete for different reasons. Some compete to gain experience while others are looking to win. Some individuals strive to be number one while others strive to be in the top ten. Winning should be defined by the individual. The one who strives to be the best will ultimately have to move into the next participation level if he or she wants to achieve the highest level of winning. Regardless of the reasons, once a person has entered the Training to Compete participation level, he is taking control of his schedule and making training a priority.

The Training to Compete level of participation is not for the wishful thinker. It is for the person serious about getting better at what he does and being willing to make sacrifices to achieve goals at a higher level. Training to Compete, in sport, will force a person to increase his training intensity. This person is also one who spends regular time with his instructor, coach, or mentor. He competes on a regular basis and invests in better equipment than the Training to Learn person. This person may win competitions, but there is one participation level that puts this person at a disadvantage.

Participation Level #3: Training to Win

There comes a time when competing isn't enough. Most Olympic Champions didn't win the Olympics without winning at smaller levels, but most athletes experienced a time when winning small events was not challenging enough. They realized that going to the Olympics and going there to win were two separate issues.

For many, most will say they want to train to win, but often they fall short. If you have ever been around passionate Olympic athletes you will see that they will do things with greater energy and emotion than their competitors. The harsh reality of sports is that some will fall short. Some will train hard and do everything right and still not make it to the Olympic Gold Medal podium. This does not mean that they are failures; it means that these individuals realize that if you are going to go for something that is extremely important you leave nothing to chance.

I have met many inspiring athletes, some who have made it and some who fell just short of making it. I can tell you the ones who competed at this participation level had no regrets. For those who fell short, they still held their head high and said, "I did everything I could to excel. I had a good career. I just didn't win everything I wanted." For those that reached the top of the mountain, they expressed their journey with passion and excitement to others.

I see many younger athletes say that they are at the

Training to Win participation level, but when you do a close evaluation of how they train and question their drive, you will find that it closely represents the second level and not the third. The difference is passion. While all three participation levels require some form of passion, it's in the Training to Win level that we see this passion shine. Athletes at this participation level don't just talk the talk, they walk the walk. These individuals hold themselves accountable, while others wait for an outside influence to help motivate them and push them to success.

Taking Control

The Training to Win participation level begins when the individual takes control, accountability and responsibility for his training and success. He becomes more adamant about his time and who he spends it with. He controls his time based on priorities and not by outside environmental distractions. He may spend up to six days a week training, scheduling his training process in advance. This individual knows what his schedule looks like for the year and has a sense of urgency that is unlike his average competitor.

Elite Performers manage their time and stick to a schedule. Others mismanage their time and do not have a schedule.

Controlling your time is an absolute must if you want to achieve your ultimate performance and see the results you should actually have. Mismanaging time is a major rea-

ELEMENT #2

Elite Performers manage their time and stick to a schedule. Others mismanage their time and do not have a schedule.

son why good performers never reach the elite level. They allow the environment to control their schedule. If you want to reach higher levels of achievement, you must make managing your time a priority.

Think about the people that you work with. How many of them spend time around the water cooler talking about what happened yesterday? Think about your teammates at practice. How many of them are focused on the task compared to the ones that are busy talking about something that is unimportant? How much time are they wasting during the day that they could be spending on focusing on the task at hand? If you are practicing or working on something important and another individual comes up to you and starts talking about unimportant things, that person is stealing your time and keeping you from accomplishing the work you should be completing.

English author Charles Buxton said, "You will never 'find' time for anything. If you want time you must make it." He is 100 percent correct. You must make time for the important things in your life. If you don't make time for the things that are important to you, you will fall victim to outside sources that will steal your time away from you. Your true potential lies within your ability to organize your time and use it wisely.

There are only 168 hours in a week. That sounds like a lot of time, but when you start to look at how your time is spent, you quickly realize that it's not enough time. If you sleep eight hours per night, like the average person, you have already used 56 of those 168 hours. You are now left with 112 hours, which still sounds like a lot of time. You might ask yourself, "Who cannot get what he needs done in 112 hours?" Let's take a look at how fast that time is consumed.

First, let's start with time spent on our everyday needs. If you use an hour to get ready for each day, i.e. shower, dress, eat breakfast and make sure you have everything you need before you head out the door, and an hour to wind down before going to sleep, you have spent another 14 hours of your 112 left. Now take the drive time you have to and from work, school, or practice. That could easily be another hour or two a day, and that does not count the hour you take for lunch. Now you are faced with about 88 hours left. Of those 88 hours, you will spend 40 hours at work or school, which leaves you with 48 hours a week or about seven hours a day to manage the other responsibilities and activities life throws at you; things like, family, TV time, exercise, friends, errands, checking email, and training.

After looking at how fast the time goes by, you can see why the elite performer has an advantage. He is able to take the time he has and organize it well. The key difference between the elite performer and his competitor is that the elite performer takes control of his time and plans out his objectives and activities each day, sometimes even weeks and months in advance.

The athletes at the Olympic Training Center know their schedule. Ask any of them what they are doing next Wednesday at 2 p.m. and they will be able to tell you. They know what they are doing every minute of the day. Many of them track their performance and keep a daily log. They keep track of their training, fitness and nutrition and look for progress in each area. It takes a very disciplined person to beat you when you take this kind of control over your schedule. This is why they do it, to give themselves an advantage that increases their chances of winning.

The Training to Win person is the one that is willing to put everything on the line while knowing that he may not reach his ultimate goal. He does not care about the end result as much as he cares about being prepared to reach it when the opportunity presents itself. He knows and trusts that if he prepares properly that he will reach his goals. This is a different type of individual; this is the one you should fear. If you have high expectations and you are not in this level, you need to be!

So ask yourself the question again. What participation level am I? Does my participation level equal my goals? If not, I need to change my goals or my participation level. Properly evaluating your participation level and managing your time will provide you with a firm grasp of the goals you should strive for.

CHAPTER 2 - OPPORTUNITY

We may never see the greatest baseball player, the greatest soccer player, the greatest golfer, or even the greatest entrepreneur. Why? Because one must have the opportunity to do something in order to succeed. Wayne Gretzky would not be, "The Great One" if he did not live in the North where hockey was popular. He would not have made it without the support and ability of his parents driving him to all his practices and games. He was given the opportunity to play hockey and he had the passion to make something of it. He took advantage of what he had, while many players of his time did not.

You have to have the opportunity, or a way to get the opportunity in order to see how great you can truly be. The reason I was able to win twelve national titles and the World CISM Championships was because I had the opportunity to train effectively every day. My parents provided me with the proper equipment and a good place to train. Without them, I would not have made it in my sport. The

University of Texas in El Paso provided me the opportunity to continue my shooting career in college. I received a full four-year athletic scholarship in rifle shooting. That scholarship allowed me the ability to train while focusing on my education.

After college, the United States Army provided me the opportunity to continue my career by allowing me to train at the United States Army Marksmanship Unit in Fort Benning, GA. They not only gave me the opportunity to train, but they gave me the opportunity to gain international experience by shooting on the US Army International Rifle Team. I was also able to represent my country on the US National Team during 1994 to 2002. With this support I was able to accomplish things that would have been impossible on my own. Nobody is able to make it by themselves; it takes a support group to provide them with the opportunity they need in order to succeed.

You need people in order to succeed

All of the successful people I have met in my life didn't get to the top by themselves. They had support from other people. You need to make sure that you have the following:

- Time
- Effort
- Resources
- People

You need to have the time to do what you desire, you

need to be willing to put in the effort, you need to have the resources to pay for the things you need, and lastly, you need to have the right people in place for you to perform at an elite level.

Having a support group around you makes life easier in ways that cannot be measured. You need someone to help you control your schedule and your technical progress. You need a mentor to help you succeed and encourage you when you hit roadblocks along the way. You need someone to help you financially as well as keep you on track with your goals. Sure, you can do some of these things by yourself, but you can't do everything alone. Your job is to surround yourself with the right support group that increases the probability of your success.

When I look back, I realize how fortunate I was. Many of the athletes that I work with are fortunate to have the necessary support they need for them to have the chance to succeed. Finding opportunity isn't easy, but it's not impossible if you have the passion and willingness to search for it. There is no better example of this than the stories of Michael Gross and Richard Lane.

I'm ninety-nine percent sure you have never heard of Michael Gross, but you may be familiar with Richard Lane. The stories of these two individuals show what creating opportunity is all about. If you desire to do more with your life, you must either take advantage of the opportunity that is in front of you, or create an opportunistic situation.

Taking no is not an option

Michael Gross was a rifle shooter in the 1970's who dreamed of making the US Team. He wanted to wear the red, white, and blue just once and proudly shoot for his country. He had recently graduated from college when he called the "International Shooting School" and spoke with my father about training at the school. Michael had one problem; he lacked the necessary funds needed in order to reach his goal. My dad had explained to him that the school didn't have a scholarship fund and that he would not be able to help him.

Two weeks went by since the phone call from Michael when we heard a knock at the front door. We were having a late dinner that evening and we looked at each other in disbelief. We never had anyone knock at our front door. We lived on a one hundred and five acre ranch, and it was a good 500 yards from the house to the gated front entrance. Who in the world would be knocking at our front door? My father got up and opened the door and there stood a winded and tired young man. "Mr. Bassham, my name is Michael Gross, I spoke with you two weeks ago. I thought a lot about what you said, so I packed up all my belongings and all my money and I drove here nonstop for the past two days. I have no money, my car ran out of gas two miles down the road, and I haven't eaten anything in 24 hours, I'm now your problem."

I would have loved to have seen the look on my dad's face when he heard those words from Michael. He let Michael in, we fed him dinner, and took him back to retrieve his car. During the next several months Michael trained at the school and worked on the ranch. He focused on shooting air rifle six days a week for up to four hours a day. He spent another four to five hours a day doing odd jobs on the ranch to pay for his stay. He became a part of the family during that time and everyone who met him immediately liked him.

By the time the nationals came around he was shooting the best scores of his life. He was as ready to make his first US National team as he could have been. It was a three-day event and Michael didn't shoot very well the first day. It wasn't a bad score, but to make the US team he needed to be on his A-game all three days. The second day faired a little better, but still it was short of what he needed in order to be in a good position to make the team. That evening no one was in a very talkative mood. We had a quiet dinner at a local restaurant near the hotel. No one was saying much of anything, which was quite unusual for the Bassham family. Michael looked up and asked, "What do I have to shoot tomorrow to make the team?" My father went on to tell him how proud he was and that he had done something that many people would never have the guts to do. Michael paused, looked up with a serious look in his eye and repeated his question. "What do I have to shoot tomorrow to make the team?" My dad replied, "Michael, you would have to shoot a national record to have any chance of making the team. No one has shot 597 or higher out of a maximum of 600. You should be proud of what you have done."

On the final day my father set up his spotting scope behind Michael. He watched Michael shoot a nine on his first shot, followed by another nine on his second shoot, and a third nine after that. My dad got up and went to watch one of his other students. I'm sure he felt disappointed for Michael. He was a good guy and sometimes things just aren't meant to be. When Michael finished, my dad and I went over to see how he did. Before you hand in your targets, every shooter tallies his score so he has a good idea of what his official score should be.

My dad took the 60 targets and immediately put the first three targets aside; he knew what they were. As he organized the remaining 57 targets, stacking them together I could see the table through the hole in the targets. My dad looked up with a grin at Michael and said, "You just made the team." Michael had shot 57 tens in a row and set a new National Record in the process. He made the team and won a silver medal at the World Championships in 1979. He quit shooting after that, but his story remains one that proves you should never give up on your dreams.

Ask and you may receive

If you're a die-hard NFL fan you know Richard Lane as Dick "Night Train" Lane. This individual is regarded as the most feared defensive back in NFL history. He still holds the record for the most interceptions by a rookie, and ranks third all-time with 68 career interceptions. He had the type of career that most players would only dream of having. He not only set records, but his style of play would force the NFL to change the rules. He was one of the most, if not the most, successful football player never to have been drafted, and that is why you need to know the rest of the story.

It's amazing that Lane survived to even touch a football. He was found at three months old in a dumpster by Ella Lane, a widow who already had two children of her own. She rescued Richard and raised him as part of her family. He went on to play high school and junior college football. He would later join the Army and serve in World War II and the Korean War. After his time in the Army, Lane grew depressed with his employment situation and decided to take action.

In 1952, he walked into the offices of the defending champion, the Los Angeles Rams, and asked for a tryout. All Lane had of his accomplishments were some clippings in his scrapbook from high school and junior college. Amazingly, head coach Joe Stydahar took a look at his scrapbook and granted him a tryout. Imagine that! The head coach of the defending champions actually granted a tryout to an unknown individual off the street. Richard Lane not only took advantage of the opportunity to tryout, but he sought out advice from great players on the team, like Tom Fears. He made sure he was going to take full advantage of this opportunity. That is exactly what he did.

Dick "Night Train" Lane became an immediate impact on the defense of the Los Angeles Rams. He played for nine years and was named to seven Pro Bowls. All of this happened because he was willing to do the one thing many

ELEMENT #3
*Elite Performers focus on opportunities.
Others focus on obstacles.*

fail to do, take advantage of the opportunity that is given. If these two stories do not inspire you to take full advantage of what you have, then what on earth will?

*Elite Performers focus on opportunities.
Others focus on obstacles.*

Ask yourself, am I taking FULL advantage of the opportunity I have been presented with? Look around at your surroundings and you will see people talking about the problems they face. They will complain about the obstacles in front of them and focus on why they are not having the success they desire. It would have been easy for Michael Gross to just give up shooting and sell his equipment and look for a job, but he didn't. He came up with a plan to make his dream happen. Dick Lane could have focused on why things were so bad and why he was not getting better work and more money. Instead, he focused on a plan and did something about his situation.

The focus that drives top performers to the elite level is their commitment to taking advantage of the opportunities they are given. If the opportunity is not there, they find a way to create it. The discovery of opportunity can be as important as the opportunity itself. This is why one must possess the passion along with the opportunity to truly expect to be able to reach their goals. Without passion, Gross and Lane would not have been motivated enough to seek out the opportunity that they created for themselves. Some will have the passion, but not the opportunity, while others will have the opportunity but not the passion. It takes both to succeed.

Are you taking advantage of the opportunities in front of you? Do you take your opportunities seriously enough to do the things others will not? The answer has to be yes in order for you to achieve success. Opportunity should be the moment you look forward to, and it should be the motivator for you to do the necessary things you need to do in order to perform at an elite level.

When obstacles occur, look at it as nothing more than an opportunity to take a negative and turn it into a positive. Every obstacle, every situation you find yourself in, and every hand you are dealt in life is an opportunity to grow. The question is, are you using these obstacles as opportunities to challenge yourself and see what you are capable of doing? Or are you using these obstacles as reasons why you cannot reach your goal?

Michael Gross never let the obstacles of not having the money and support he needed get in the way of making something happen. He created a plan and acted on it. He had no idea how things were going to turn out. He took a chance, and when he was presented with the opportunity to train at the shooting school, he took advantage of it with full force. He never complained about not having the opportunity earlier. He never complained about working on the ranch and doing range maintenance. He kept his focus on what he had and how he was progressing. This is the fundamental difference between those who reach their top ability and those who fall short.

Obstacles serve a purpose. If you have big dreams and goals, you will be presented with many obstacles and problems. If you focus negatively on your particular problems, you will find plenty of excuses and reasons as to why you are not successful. If you put your mental energy on what kind of opportunities are being presented and remain positive, you can turn a difficult situation into a great turning point in your career. This is what Michael Gross and Dick Lane did. They turned a difficult situation into an opportunity that led to success. If you have an opportunity to succeed, take advantage of it. If you don't have the opportunity, find a way to create it!

Adversity is an Opportunity

An individual must take advantage of the opportunity that is given to him or her. In the beginning this is easy. Everyone is motivated in the beginning and they are focused on what they like about the opportunity that is in front of them. The difficult part comes when problems arise.

When faced with difficult situations, problems can begin to occupy our thoughts. It's human nature to allow our conscious mind to drift more to what we don't like instead of being mentally disciplined to focus on the opportunity at hand. In order to increase the chances of taking advantage of the opportunity you have, you must view problems as a positive. Problems show areas of necessary growth. If you are not having any problems or challenges, chances are you are setting your goals too low.

Sometimes you have to broaden your opportunity and

do things that others would think is extreme. Leif Rolland is a perfect example of this. Leif and I have been friends for years, and we were competitors from the 1990's to 2002. He was the best Air Rifle shooter Norway had at that time and he would go on to compete in three Olympic Games, win 10 World Cup medals and hold the World record twice.

Leif had a dream to compete in the Olympics, and rifle shooting was going to be his ticket there. The issue was how he was going to have the opportunity to shoot. His parents didn't have the finances to support his shooting and his dad didn't have the time to drive him to the range to practice. At thirteen years of age Leif broadened his opportunity by coming up with ways to make his dream happen. He started working to earn money to pay for his shooting. On days that he could not get a ride to the range, he walked the two miles both ways, with his shooting bag over his shoulder. On days that he couldn't get to the range, he would dry-fire at home and work on his hold. Leif's other issue was that he was too young to have a key to the range, so many times he had to wait for an adult to show up before he could start his practice. Every day he would ask the range manager for a set of keys, while also showing how responsible he could be. Later the manager gave Leif his own set of keys.

Accepting your situation for what it is will not generate the opportunity necessary for you to win at the elite level. You must broaden your opportunity and make things happen, no matter how old you are. Leif did not let his age or his situation stop him from becoming an elite performer.

Instead, he used this adversity to broaden his opportunity. The question for you is do you do the same?

An aspect of elite performance is the ability to perform in tough situations when problems arise. Anyone can perform well when things are going well. It's when you are faced with tough situations that you determine if you can perform at an elite level. Michael Gross could have spent hours complaining about fixing fences and cleaning horse stables in the afternoon. What made him successful was his attitude toward his opportunity. He always focused on the good and never complained about the bad. Anything worth achieving in life will almost always present you with tough situations. What do you focus on, the good or the bad?

Every situation is an opportunity for success, no matter how big or how small it is. If you're in a competition and you find yourself starting out poorly, it's not a bad day. It's an opportunity to comeback and finish strong. By having this type of attitude you take away the winning and losing and turn it into winning and learning.

You either win or learn. There is no losing.

Every competition has a winner, but is doesn't mean that everyone else is a loser. You only lose in a situation when you don't win or learn something in the process. If you find yourself in defeat and you do not take a learning lesson from it, then at that moment you have lost. You have lost the opportunity to learn something that could make you better at what you do. You have lost the opportunity to grow and challenge yourself to keep moving forward. And you have lost the opportunity to grow as an individual, which is a necessary ingredient to reaching higher levels of success.

In order to grow, you must constantly look for ways to get better at the things you do. It is an ongoing process that is common to elite performers. They consistently look for ways to grow in areas that will increase the chances of their being successful. They will focus on getting better at all levels. This includes their areas of strength.

John Wooden, the famous UCLA college basketball coach who has won more games than any other basketball coach in history, said that the thing that separates the great player from the good player is that the good player works on his weaknesses and that the great player works on his strengths. The elite performer focuses on strengths and then focuses on his weaknesses. He makes it a point to focus on how he can improve and grow. Elite performers don't focus on excuses, nor do they focus on winning or losing. The elite performer focuses on progress, and he takes advantage of his opportunities.

CHAPTER 3 - TRAINING WITH PURPOSE

If there is one area that is more challenging than all the others, it has to be training with a purpose. Training with a specific purpose sounds logical, but it's amazing how many people fail to set specifics on what they should work on throughout the day. If you are going to reach high levels of achievement, then you must stay on top of what you have mastered. That means doing things that may not be fun, but are required in order to achieve the results you desire.

Training with a purpose starts with an objective solely focused on the things you must do for that day. No great athlete goes to practice without objectives, but there are many athletes who go to practice without a detailed objective for the day. By having specific objectives laid out in advance it allows the individual to have structure while keeping him accountable and making his training more efficient. Without these objectives the individual is just practicing and not getting the full benefit of their time.

Objectives in training must have specific drills and a detailed training regiment that emphasizes the things one must master in order to become really good. Purposeful practice sets in when the individual is willing to do what is necessary even when he knows it may not be something that he enjoys doing.

To get a better idea, let's take a close look at how the South Koreans train their Olympic Archers. When they receive a young individual who wants, and initially shows some passion for the sport, they introduce the individual to the sport differently than other countries. For starters, they begin by having the new archer learn the basic idea of form by taking a special rubber band and simulating proper drawing form used with a bow. The individual archer will face a mirror in order to see what proper head placement should look like while focusing on the muscles that are being used. The purpose of this exercise is for the archer to learn the proper form of shooting, while building up the proper muscles before allowing him or her the opportunity to shoot.

These young archers perform this type of training for three to six months. Once they have the form down they move into the second level of shooting. At this level they get to shoot with a bow using the same form they worked on with the rubber band. They do not get to shoot at a target; instead they shoot at a blank bale. The focus here is to teach proper hand placement on the bow while implementing the proper draw and release of the shot. Once this technique is mastered they are able to move on to the third level.

By the time a young archer has reached the third level, he or she may have spent up to eight months learning proper form. At this level, the archer will start with the target at a close distance of 30 meters. This improves his or her likelihood of them hitting the center of the target and getting some good results. Once each shooter can consistently shoot at this distance, the coach will increase the weight of the bow. The focus is to get each shooter to a certain technical skill level before allowing him or her to move on to the next level. This type of focus and purposeful training works because it protects all three areas of performance: the Conscious Mind, the Subconscious Mind and the Self-Image.

The Three areas of Performance

If you have read "With Winning in Mind" you have a good idea of how performance is generated. Performance consists of three mental processes: the Conscious Mind, the Subconscious Mind, and the Self-Image. Most individuals focus on building the Subconscious, but you must focus on all three if you truly expect to reach your highest level of performance.

The Conscious Mind controls your thoughts. Every time you smell, hear, taste, see, or touch something you do it consciously. The Conscious Mind is like your periscope. It gathers information about what's around you. It's active, and it is limited in its ability because the conscious mind can only think about one thing at a time. Can you be positive and negative at the same time? Can you be happy and sad at the same time? Can you think about winning and losing at the same time? Of course not! You can only focus on one of these areas at a time. This is why it is difficult to master a new activity from the start.

There are so many things that your Conscious Mind is trying to think about that it cannot possibly process them all. When you first learn something new you have to perform it consciously because you have yet to develop the proper skill necessary to perform the task well. There are so many things to master that the Conscious Mind is unable to keep up. Therefore you must practice the basics over and over in order to gain skill. Skill is developed through repetitive practice until the Subconscious Mind can take over. The important thing to know is that the Conscious Mind plays an important role in your ability to learn a sport or activity because it helps train the subconscious mind.

The Subconscious Mind is the source of your skills and power to perform. Once the task at hand is mastered, and you can perform it without thinking about it, you have built the necessary subconscious skill to become great at your sport or activity. An example of this is tying your shoe. When is the last time you actually thought about tying your shoe? You probably cannot even remember, because you can perform the task subconsciously. However, your ability to perform can still be limited if you do not have the third area of performance built, the Self Image.

The Self-Image is what makes you act like you. It is the

sum total of your habits and attitudes. It's how an individual sees himself or herself to be. The size of your Self-Image is built on imprints from the Conscious and Subconscious Mind. This is important, because every time you think about or perform a task it affects the growth, or lack of growth, of your Self-Image. If you have success with something, your Self-Image about that task grows. In the same way, when you experience failure or beat yourself up over a failed task, your Self-Image about that task will shrink. This is how confidence is built or lost.

We have all seen really talented athletes fall short in competition. Some lack the confidence needed to perform well in competition. When this happens, the individual's performance is better in practice than in competition. It is not because he lacks the ability to perform, but rather because he lacks the confidence and appropriate Self Image to perform at a high level. Simply put, if you think I can beat you and I think I can beat you, what chance do you have at winning? You have little to no chance at all.

Elite Performers work on all three areas of performance. Others focus only on their subconscious ability.

When it comes to purposeful practice, one must work on all three areas of performance if he truly expects to reach high levels of achievement. We see far too many athletes train on only the Subconscious Mind. If this happens they will fall short in competition because they lack the neces-

ELEMENT #4

Elite Performers work on all three areas of performance. Others focus only on their subconscious ability.

sary skills in the Conscious Mind and the Self Image. You must focus on building each of these areas of performance in training. The best way to do this is to incorporate the three training phases into your training week.

The Three Training Areas

There are three ways to break down your training. If you are in a team sport, your coaches already do this to some degree. They make you work on skills and have you perform different drills to increase your technical ability. They have you run certain plays, memorize strategies that will be implemented in the game. They also remind you to focus and to stay in the moment. Leave out one of these essential elements and your game suffers The only way to grow and reach success is to incorporate skill, the mental game, and game rehearsal into your training.

Train for Feel

Anytime we learn something new, we must first master the basics. We can never expect to become great at anything until we have the basic foundation built. In this way, it is necessary to start with training for feel. This area of training focuses on the quantity of training over the quality of training. The purpose of training for feel is to get the feel down of what we are trying to master. This is done by using different types of drills to get our bodies to do what we want without having to consciously think about it.

When I first started shooting, I didn't get to shoot like everyone else. In the beginning, I started out shooting an air rifle with support. I used a kneeling roll to rest the rifle on the bench to keep the rifle stable. The purpose of this was to get a feel of what proper sight alignment and sight picture should look like. For a beginner, it's impossible to hold the rifle well enough to shoot the target, let alone the ten ring. By resting the rifle on the kneeling roll it allowed for the rifle to be steady and I was able to learn proper sight alignment, sight picture, and trigger control.

Once the basic understanding is done, you need to build on your foundation. In shooting, this is done by working on learning the proper shooting positions. In air rifle, we shoot the standing position from 33 feet away using iron sights. The rifle is constantly moving and it is very difficult for the new shooter to shoot in the middle. The purpose of training for feel is to get the athlete to understand and master some foundational skills. This type of training will never go away in any athlete's career, but it will be more intense in the beginning as the subconscious skill is being developed.

In order for me to develop a good standing position, I spent many hours a day dry firing and group shooting. Dry firing is when you shoot without a bullet. This allows the shooter to focus on proper position and not on results. Group shooting is when a shooter will shoot several shots before looking at the target. The purpose of this is to allow the shooter an opportunity to shoot live rounds without seeing the shots until after several shots have been fired. This type of training is important because it protects and builds up the Self-Image.

What you want to accomplish in training for feel is to develop and work on subconscious ability while also protecting the Self-Image. I see many athletes play, but not train. In golf, many players will spend more time out on the course than on the driving range or putting green. They focus more on results rather than on their progress and development. To be great, you need both. If you are working on a technical issue, training for feel is the best form of practice you can utilize. Once you have mastered the technique you are ready for the next area of training.

Train for the Task

No matter what you are trying to master there are specific tasks that require both technical and mental aspects in order to become proficient. A person cannot just focus on trying to execute the technical part of the task and expect to be able to perform that task well when it truly counts. To get a better understanding of this I will use golf as an example, but the following lesson will apply to any activity you are trying to master.

For a golfer, training for the task is referred to as training for the shot. This is when the golfer will break down what he is physically and mentally doing in order to improve the opportunity to execute the shot he wants. This form of training focuses more on quality and less on quantity. The player will focus on running his pre-shot routine while simultaneously executing the technical shot he wants to perform. We see this with elite golfers most frequently.

In order to train the mind and the body at the same

time, a player needs to simulate what he wants to execute on the course while he is at the driving range. He can't expect to go out and play well if he hasn't mentally prepared. This type of training prepares him to warm up both mentally and physically. When a player is hitting a lot of golf balls and is working on a specific shot, it's all about training for feel. Once he gets that shot down, he will need to incorporate an effective mental system to accompany it. This is where training for the shot comes into practice.

Instead of spending hours hitting ball after ball, the player will spend hours in this phase practicing his pre-shot routine and running his mental program. Here is an example of that process. First the player picks a specific target on the range and selects the right club. He then takes a ball, and instead of hitting the shot, he steps back and goes through his mental process while simulating what he would do if he were on the course. This allows the player to work on fine tuning his mental program and pre-shot routine so that it will stay consistent once he goes out on the course and plays for score.

If the player doesn't focus on this type of training, he or she increases the chances of making mental errors on the course. This type of training forces the individual to concentrate on the specific task at hand and reduces the chances of just going through the motions. If a player doesn't practice his mental game in training, how can he expect to be prepared for the competition? I will break this down into more detail in the next chapter.

Train for the Event

Training for the event is taking the next step after training for the task. In shooting, we refer to this as training for the match, whereas in golf it is referred to as training for the round, and in basketball it's referred to as training for the game, etc. The purpose of this form of training is to simulate exactly what you want to do in competition, when it counts. Just like the example of the golfer before, he can't expect to play well in a tournament if he doesn't spend time playing rounds in practice as if he were in actual competition. During this period of training, the individual is simulating how he would execute his course management, mental process, and technical game under tournament conditions.

You must role-play in practice exactly how you want to do in the real event before you can expect to execute it perfectly in a competition. This form of training is designed to include all aspects of performance; mental, physical, and technical. It requires the individual to focus like he or she would in a real life situation. This overall training will not provide the same type of intensity as a tournament would, but if you don't incorporate it into your weekly training schedule, you will not be mentally prepared to handle the pressure in competition.

Elite Performers train with a purpose.
Others practice what they enjoy.

ELEMENT #5

*Elite Performers train with a purpose.
Others practice what they enjoy.*

No matter which area of training you are focusing on, you want to make sure you are working on the necessary areas to improve your performance. This means continually working on your strengths and weaknesses. Training with a purpose is having a plan to work on all aspects of your game to better prepare you for success. All too often many of us get sidetracked. By having a plan, the necessary tools to improve and a plan on how to use them, you reduce the risk of falling short on your objectives.

Having a weekly training plan and making sure we focus on the right things is the best way to handle training with purpose. Training with purpose is accomplished by adhering to a weekly training plan that helps you focus on the correct areas of improvement. The training plan must diagram which days you are taking off and state specific objectives for your days of training or competing. Top performers value their time and are not willing to let anything get in the way of them being better prepared. They keep track of their training plan and make proper adjustments from week to week.

Training with a purpose means that your training schedule should be built in a way to help you improve all three areas of performance. All too often we focus on building skill and not on protecting our Self-Image. You need to have a schedule that gives you the best chance of having a successful training day. This starts by organizing your training in a way that allows you to start off with success and end with success.

When I'm working with athletes, I want them to identify their specific strengths and weaknesses. I do this to organize their training based on protecting their Self-Image first and then building their subconscious ability second. This works really well in individual sports. If you have three specific areas in which you are going to practice one day, how you organize the order of training can be the difference between improving quickly or developing slowly. You need to follow the basic Three Step Training Rule.

Three Step Training Rule:

The main purpose of the Three Step Training Rule is to work on technical skill and improve confidence at the same time. You must protect your Self-Image while improving your ability. This type of training allows you to do both.

The first step is to always start your training session with success. To improve the likelihood that you will start off with success, always begin your training with an area of strength. This helps build confidence in the Self-Image. After you start off your practice with an area of strength, you will have an attitude focused on success. This attitude will carry over to your practice and put you in the right mindset for an effective training session.

The second step is to always work on your weak areas during the middle part of your training session. Make sure to start easy and work your way up to the harder part of your training. This approach protects your self-image while building the necessary subconscious skills needed to perform at a higher level.

The final step is to always end with success. Save your

best strength and practice it last. If you're a golfer and putting is the strongest part of your game, then it should be the last thing you practice. This step improves the likelihood of ending on a positive note. The purpose for organizing your training in this manner is to allow for a more effective and efficient training day.

The three step-training rule works well because you are always focused on the areas of strength and your areas of weakness throughout your period of training. By sandwiching the "needs work" areas between your strengths, you're helping to build and protect your Self-Image. The time you spend on the "needs work" areas should be longer than the time you spend on the strengths. For example, if you have two hours for a training session in golf and you have determined that you need to focus on three areas of development, you would organize your time accordingly:

30 minutes on your first area of strength
1 hour on your "needs work" area
30 minutes on your second area of strength

Change it up

If you have a situation occur where you are not having a good practice session, change up the practice. Sometimes moving onto another area of training and then re-visiting the problem can help alter your mindset and allow for a more effective training session. This will keep you focused on training your subconscious ability while at the same time reducing the frustration level that comes when you are faced with a bad training day.

The goal is to always have success. It does little good to keep practicing something that is not going well. By changing up the practice, you will be more likely to have a positive training session. Once the training session is over, always focus on what went well. No matter how poor some days appear to be, there are always things that you are doing well and it is important to focus on those. Make sure you credit yourself for your successes. Remember, changing up the practice doesn't mean that you don't work on the areas that need work. Changing it up means that you move onto something else and then come back to the area that was not working well before. You will be amazed how many times you perform better the second time around.

When things are going well, extend the practice session

When things are going well, extend your practice. If you are practicing putting and you are putting well, keep on putting. The successful imprints from continuously putting well are helping to build your Self-Image and increase your confidence. Many athletes spend little time on their areas of strength and focus more on their areas of weakness. Remember, that when you are performing above average keep on going. This rule will help you develop all areas quicker and make your training more fun and productive.

CHAPTER 4 - BECOME MENTALLY STRONG

Success, in any form, is rarely an accident. Sure, there are examples of someone being successful where luck plays a role, but to truly reach the top level of your ability you must put yourself in a position to be lucky. You can't simply wait for success to happen, you must strive for it and take advantage of your position. No one can determine the success they will have. You can only move toward the success you desire and prepare yourself to take advantage of the situations that come your way.

In order to reach the next level of success that you desire, you must become mentally strong in your thought process. You must think about what you want and not give into the temptation of thinking about why you don't have it. The conscious mind is powerful and it can lead you into the direction of being the person you want to be. You have heard the saying, "You are what you eat," well, I'm telling you that you become what you think!

If you think you won't win, you're right. It's that simple.

The thoughts we have about ourselves will lead us toward being that person. It doesn't matter how good you are, if you think you don't have a chance to win, you won't win. Certainly you must posses the necessary skills in order to be competitive to win. If you're reading this book, chances are the skill level you posses is not the deciding factor of why you're not successful.

No successful person ever made it by not thinking about what it takes to become successful. All flourishing individuals have thought about being successful. This is a three-part process. Part one is to think about being successful. Part two is to think about how to become successful. The third part is to duplicate the process once you have reached success. Do you think Donald Trump spends him time worrying why certain business deals did not get done? No, he spends his time focusing on the successful deals that he made and how he can duplicate that success.

In order to achieve, you must acquire the correct thought process.

You must acquire the ability to think properly in order to achieve the results you desire. We live in a world where the environment pulls our conscious thoughts away from us. Too often we allow things to bother us rather than ignoring the unimportant things and choosing to think about what is truly important. Far too many people concentrate and spend countless hours fabricating excuses and reasons why they are not having the success they want. Instead, they need to spend their mental energy on what they should be doing in order to achieve the results they desire.

An individual's way of doing something is a direct result of the way he or she thinks.

If you strive to be successful, you must control your thoughts. A classic example of how top performers differ from the other participants is how they think in problematic situations. Ask yourself one simple but extremely important question. Am I spending my time thinking about the soution to the problem, or am I spending my time thinking about the problem itself? If you have any desire to excel you will encounter problems. If you keep focusing on problems, you will improve the likelihood of having more problems. In order to get closer to your goals you must focus on the solutions to the issues and not continue to dwell on areas of concern.

*Elite Performers focus on Solutions.
Others focus on problems.*

Everyone who strives to be successful will have to overcome problems and obstacles. How you approach your thoughts on issues will determine the path you take toward success. What makes elite performers unique is their ability to focus on solutions to their problems. Most people will complain and focus on the issue at hand, while successful people are solution oriented with their thoughts.

Every person has the natural and inherent power to

ELEMENT #6
*Elite Performers focus on Solutions.
Others focus on problems.*

control his or her thoughts. Our experiences may help to generate how we think about certain topics and the way we live, but regardless of past experiences we have the ability to think any way we desire. Having the mental discipline to think in a certain way that will lead us to become who we desire to be is critical to reaching success. This type of thought process is a key ingredient that separates winners from competitors.

Many of us think about being successful. Generally, it is not the initial thought about success that fails us, but the lack of discipline to choose the necessary thought process in order to achieve the success that we intend. Growing up around successful athletes, I learned that they rarely thought the same way other athletes did. They had a way of thinking that was different and it gave them an advantage over their competition.

The Principle of Reinforcement states, "The more you think about, talk about, and write about something happening you improve the probability of that thing happening." The first part of this principle is key; the more you think about something happening, the more you improve the probability of it actually happening.

No one ever gets to the top without having a vision of being great. You cannot become the best teacher, athlete, salesman, or manager without having the thoughts of being great at what you do. Every time you think about what you want, it creates an imprint into your Self-Image that brings you one step closer to achieving your goal.

In order to reach high levels of achievement you must

ELEMENT #7
*Elite Performers focus on what they should do.
Others focus on what happened.*

think about what it takes to get there, and you must think about it often. This form of thinking is important; it's the key principle of creating and building the Self-Image you need in order to achieve the goals you have set. I could not have become the best rifle shooter in the nation without having a plan and believing that I could someday make that goal happen. You cannot achieve your goals if you do not think about what you want and how you are going to get there. This is a mental skill that must be developed and become a habit. Top performers are very good at this. You must develop a plan and believe in the plan before you can achieve your goal.

Elite Performers focus on what they should do. Others focus on what happened.

It's hard to make this thought process a habit. Often times, it is far easier to think about what you want and why you might not have it, compared to what you want and how you can achieve it.

In the spring of 1998 I missed the World Championship team by one tenth of a point. I was devastated! Instead of shooting against the best in the world I was going to have to compete at the NRA National Championships. I remember complaining to my wife, Frances, about missing this opportunity and failing to meet my goal of being the best. She calmly told me that I could still be the best in the nation and that I should focus on that, instead of feeling sorry for myself. I was mad! I did not want to be the best in the country; I wanted to be the best in the world. I told her that even if I won the Nationals that many would say it did not count because the top Americans would all be competing at the World Championships. My wife looked at me in the eye and said, "I guess you'll just have to set a national record!"

I was thinking about the environment and not on my performance. My goal in shooting was to be the best. I cannot control what others did, and I certainly could not guarantee the career I would have. All of my teammates had the same goal as I did, and the reality was that some were going to have better careers than others. I was failing to think about the process I needed to follow in order to be the best shooter I could be. The next day I started focusing on what I needed to do to win the NRA Nationals. As a result of my thought process I changed my training, and what followed was my success. I won the National Championships that summer with a new national record. The following year I would repeat as National Champion and win the 300 Meter World Championships in Standard Rifle.

What happened to me wasn't important. How I responded to my circumstances was important. For me I was lucky to have my wife remind me of what I needed to do. If she had not been there to refocus me at that time I would have complained to others and felt bad about my situation. I see this happen all too often with young athletes. As soon as they don't get what they want they complain and ask why instead of focusing on what needs to be done. If you don't have what you want and you are complaining about your situation then you have what you deserve.

It is easy to focus and talk about what happened. A better way of spending that mental energy is to focus on what you should have done and not on what you did. With this type of thought process you have the chance of reaching the success you desire.

Staying focused on what you need to do in order to overcome the obstacles in front of you is another main ingredient to attaining success. You may have never heard of Karoly Takacs, but in the 1940s he was well known in Hungary. Everyone familiar with his story has been inspired by it.

In 1938 Karoly Takacs was a Sergeant in the Army and was a top ranked pistol shooter in the world. He was a favorite to win the Olympics held in Tokyo, Japan in 1940. Karoly's goals and aspirations of being the best in the world vanished during a military training accident when a defective hand grenade exploded in his right hand - his shooting hand. In a matter of seconds he went from being one of the best to unable to shoot at all. He would spend a month in the hospital depressed at the loss of his hand and the loss of his Olympic dream.

For many people this would have been devastating. The accident and drama of losing a hand would haunt many of us for years. The easiest thing to do would be to focus on the loss and why it happened in the first place. The thoughts of feeling sorry for oneself could eventually cause some to fall into severe depression. For Karoly it was a different experience. After leaving the hospital, he secretly taught himself how to shoot with his left hand while using his right eye. Karoly did what many top performers do; he focused on what he had and made full use of his ability. What he had was a competitive spirit, experience, mental toughness, and a healthy left hand that with time would develop to be the greatest asset in his shooting career.

For months Karoly practiced by himself. No one knew what he was doing. Maybe he didn't want to subject himself to others who would discourage him. Maybe he didn't want to give false hope to his family and friends on a comeback. Or maybe it was his way of coping with his accident. For Karoly it was the right thing to do leading up to the 1939 national championships.

When Karoly Takacs showed up at the 1939 National Championships, many of his friends and other shooters greeted him with open arms and were excited that he came to watch them shoot. They were surprised when he told them that he was there to compete, and they were even more surprised when he won!

Things looked like they were back in order for Karoly. He was now the talk of the shooting communities and his dream of going to the Olympics was once again a reality. This new reality proved to be short-lived, as the 1940 and 1944 Olympics were canceled, due to World War II. It looked as though Karoly's dream of going to the Olympics was not meant to be, but he would continue his training over that eight-year period and qualify for the 1948 Olympics at the age of 38.

Before the rapid-fire pistol event, Carlos Enrique Diaz Saenz Valiente, the former World Champion and the current world record holder and favorite to win the event, asked Karoly why he was in London, England. The reply that Karoly gave was a humble one, "I am here to learn." Karoly not only won the gold medal, but he beat Carlos Valiente's world record by ten points. During the award ceremony, it is said that Carlos looked at Karoly and said, "You have learned enough." Karoly would also repeat as Olympic Gold medalist four years later in Helsinki, Finland.

The more you think about something happening, the more you improve the probability of that thing happening. This is what Karoly Takacs did better than anyone else. He never doubted what he could achieve, but focused constantly on what he needed to do in order to put himself in a position to achieve his goals. His story is one that is told throughout the international shooting communities around the world. While many will use his story as one that proves you should never give up, I think it's Karoly's ability to think about what he wanted and do what he needed to do to achieve it that is the bigger lesson learned.

Elite Performers focus on the process.
Others focus on outcome.

This is a difficult concept for many to grasp because it takes outcome out of the equation and focuses on process. Being outcome minded is good for setting goals and push-

ELEMENT #8
*Elite Performers focus on the process.
Others focus on outcome.*

ing yourself to train, but when competing, the focus must shift to being process minded.

Making process primary allows an individual to have mental consistency. It's a far easier task to focus on the results and the outcome you want compared to focusing on the execution of what you should be doing to achieve those results. In competition it is all about the process. Elite performers trust their ability and focus on execution. You must avoid thinking about results while competing.

When I was learning how to shoot my father would talk about being mentally consistent. I had to duplicate my thought process in order to shoot at my true subconscious ability. We call it running a mental program. Although the idea of this thought process makes sense, I didn't really know how to explain it until the fall of 2006.

My father and I were working together with Fred Funk, a professional golfer playing on the PGA and Champions Tour. Fred was not winning on the Champions Tour, where he was competing against the best players fifty years old and older. Fred was falling short of his potential. He had proven himself by winning on the PGA Tour before and many people felt like he would win several Champions Tour events with ease. Fred's issue was a double-edged sword: his problem was that he was not winning because he focused on the outcome of winning rather than on the process he needed to follow in order to win.

I can remember the conversation like it was yesterday. My father looked at Fred in our conference room and said, "You're so busy thinking about winning, or why you're not winning, that you're taking yourself out of a chance to win. Your job isn't to win events, but instead to follow a consistent thought process that will allow you to consistently play at your true subconscious ability." He then gave the following example.

In 1974 there were three events leading up to the World Championships. He wanted to make sure he put himself in the best position to win, so he developed a mental program; a thought process that he could repeat before each and every shot. This thought process never changed. He didn't think about what he shot, how the hold looked, or what others were doing. He focused on running his mental program. That was the priority.

During the first match, his goal was to run this new thought process at least 80 percent of the time. He didn't care about results; he only cared about running his mental program 80 percent or better. At the end of the match he did well, he ran his mental program 80 percent of the time and he won the match. The second match he improved how well he ran his mental program. He ran it 85 percent of the time and won that match. The third match he ran his mental program 90 percent of the time and won that match. He ask Fred, "What do you think I should change?"

Fred replied, "Nothing!"

In order to have mental consistency, you must find the optimal mental thought that yields the best opportunity to have a successful performance and repeat that thought process every single time. For many players, the only mental consistency they have is that they are mentally inconsistent with their thoughts. They tend to be environmentally sensitive. When looking at a tee shot and seeing water to the right, they will focus on where they don't want to hit the ball rather than following a thought process that will improve the likelihood of hitting the ball exactly where they want it to go.

Think about it. If you focus on not hitting the ball in the water, what do you picture in your mind? You picture hitting the ball into the water. What do you think the probability of hitting the ball into the water will be? According to the first fundamental thought process of successful people, the ball will end up in the water. This is why you must have the second fundamental thought process down in order to achieve what you desire.

A golfer cannot think about trouble on one tee shot and then think about crushing a driver on the next tee shot and expect to have consistency in his game. By allowing the environment to control your thought process you will automatically think about outcome and results. No matter how hard you try, you cannot control the outcome, but you can put yourself in position to have the best opportunity to create the outcome you want. The only way you can do that is to be process-minded.

Fred's inability to focus on his process was one of the things that was hurting his chances of winning. He needed to incorporate a consistent thought process that yielded the best opportunity for him to perform at his best every single time. Once he incorporated this mental program into his game, consistency followed and results started to appear. He won two of his next three Champions Tour events and followed that up with his eighth PGA Tour career win.

This thought process works in all areas of life no matter what you do for a living. In sales, you cannot control the outcome of whether someone buys from you or not. All you can do is put yourself in the best position to make the sale happen. Focus on only the areas that you can control and never worry about the things you cannot. If you are a teacher, chances are high that you do this without even knowing it. Can a math student know the answer without working through the proper steps of the equation? No. An educator's job is to show them how to approach the problem and take it one step at a time. If executed properly, the outcome will be the correct answer. Far too many people get ahead of themselves and start to focus on the results of where they are and not on what they need to do. This can be the difference between being successful and just getting by.

When the moment counts, Process is Primary.

On December 19, 2008, I awoke to my alarm clock that was set to ESPN radio and heard one of the best interviews ever. The show was Mike and Mike in the Morning. Mike Greenberg and Mike Golic were interviewing Tiger Woods and Greenberg wanted to know about the 72nd hole at the U.S. Open when Tiger needed to make birdie in order to force a playoff with Rocco Mediate. Greenberg stated that he was fascinated by the mental game of sport and he asked Tiger the following question. "When you were walking around the green, you're lining it up, setting it up. At any point did you allow the thought to go through your head, this is for the US Open, if I miss this I lose? Did you ever allow that thought to actually go through your mind?"

Tiger immediately replied, "No."

Greenberg said "Never?"

Tiger replied, "No. The putt was a ball and a half outside the right edge and I committed to releasing the putt and knocking it in."

"And that's it? You treated it like it was any other putt you might be making under any other set of circumstances?" replied Greenberg.

"You just read the putt and just putt, yeah," said Tiger.

Greenberg replied, "But how? I try to get to the bottom of this with guys like you. How do you do it? How do you not allow yourself to think that way? If I'm playing Golic for a $15 Nassau and I've got that putt to win it, my knees are knocking against each other and I can't get that thought out of my head. How do you not think about it?"

Tiger's response was, "That's why you host radio and I play golf!"

95 percent of winning is accomplished by 5 percent of the participants, and now you know why. The top performers don't think the same way everyone else does. Mike Greenberg is providing a classic example of what the average competitive person thinks about, while Tiger is providing us with a small example of how the top elite performers think. It comes down to being mentally disci-

ELEMENT #9
Elite Performers give just the right amount of effort. Others try to give it 110 percent.

plined. Tiger is treating every shot equally, and he gives no further thought or importance to one shot verses another. The average person doesn't do this. The average person thinks about and focuses on what the environment is telling him. In this example it becomes, "You need to make this or you lose!" Tiger Woods is being process minded and Mike Greenberg is being outcome minded. Which one are you?

You need to be process oriented in your thoughts or you will hold yourself back from the top-level performer that you are. This is one of the main things we focus on at Mental Management® Systems. When it comes to a specific task, like shooting, hitting a golf ball, or throwing a pitch, you need to have a consistent set of thoughts running through your mind before the action of that task. Running a mental program allows your Conscious Mind to get out of the way and lets your Subconscious Mind perform the task at hand with ease. When this is done effectively good performance is easy and consistent.

> *Elite Performers give just the right amount of effort. Others try to give it 110 percent.*

The Principle of Effort states, "Everything in life needs a certain amount of mental effort to perform a chosen task at the optimum level. If you expend one percent more or less effort than is required, performance suffers." This is a constant balancing act that one goes through mentally. Just how much effort should you give? Elite performers give just enough effort, nothing more and nothing less.

You have heard people say that you must give it 110, or 150 percent. What does that mean? If you actually gave it 110 percent, what would be the result of your effort? The end result is over-trying and this is the number one reason why people fail to perform at their top level.

I was working with a college athlete, who made the comment to me that you have to give it 110 percent or you're not pushing yourself hard enough to succeed. My response was, "Winning isn't about how hard you push yourself. Pushing yourself is what you do in training. When competing, it's a different story." The Olympic Gold medalists have a saying, "Giving 110 percent is a guaranteed way to lose." If you give it more effort than what is required you will fall short of the success you are trying to accomplish. You can't give something more than what it required and expect good results.

To prove my point, I handed my student an empty cup and a pitcher filled with water. I asked him to pour 110 percent of the water into the cup. He wouldn't do it. He said, "If I do that it will make a big mess and you will make me clean it up." My reply, "What do think is happening to you in competition?" When you give more effort than what is required your performance becomes a mess and the result is not pretty, just like the extra 10 percent of water overflowing from the cup. Conversely, if you give it less than 100 percent you're not using the cup to its full capacity.

The optimum amount of effort.

Elite performers understand the optimum amount of effort. If we give something one percent less effort than is required or one percent more than is needed, the performance drops. You must know when to push yourself, and you must know when to trust yourself. If you're doing things right, you trust in competition and try in practice, not the other way around. If you don't perform in this way, you will risk the likelihood of over-trying, and that is the number one reason good performers do not win. This is why many people fail to reach their top level of performance. They get in their own way by exerting too much effort.

There are four reasons why individuals over-try. First, they focus on the outcome over the process, causing them to give more effort than what is required. This happens often because it is so easy to get caught up and worry about the "unknowns."

If you are worried about what the result may be and not focused on the process of executing the task at hand, how likely are you to get the result you want? You cannot think about two things at once. You cannot think about the result while trying to execute the process. Your focus must be on the process and not on what the outcome may or may not be.

Secondly, most individuals fail to trust their ability. People who do not trust themselves and worry about what the result might be are individuals that are afraid to submit to their subconscious ability. This is a classic sign of an individual who does not practice enough or prepare properly. They really do not know or understand what their subconscious ability level is. When this happens, individuals will tend to be "extra careful" with their performance. Being extra careful is the same as over-trying. You are trying not to mess up and are therefore putting yourself in a position to over-think. Over-thinking leads to over-trying.

Elite performers work hard in preparation and easy in competition. If you prepare properly, you should focus on your process and trust that your ability will generate the outcome you want. The key is to work just hard enough, and trust your ability to perform.

Thirdly, most people operate on the misconception that trying harder will produce a greater chance of success. Think about the times when you performed well. How hard were you trying? How much effort were you giving? When we talk to top performers the most common answer is "not much." They tend to allow the performance to happen, while others try to make the performance happen. In order to operate with the correct amount of effort, one must have the attitude of letting it happen and not trying to make it happen.

Finally, the fourth reason occurs when you are trying to please other people. We see this occur with young performers. When a person focuses on what others think about his performance, his performance tends to suffer. You cannot think about your process while worrying about what your coach, parent, teammates, or others might think of you.

Focusing on what others think about your performance

while you're competing forces you to become unfocused. The end result will be lower than your true potential. This is a classic example of the unfocused individual. You cannot allow yourself to focus on others. You can only focus on what you can control. This is the difference between trying and trusting.

As parents, coaches, and mentors we want our athletes to focus on the task at hand. We want them to be process minded. We do not want them to focus on us or anyone else during the competition. Elite performers focus on what they can control and on how much effort is needed. They do not concern themselves with what others think about them, nor do they try to impress those around them. The task at hand and the effort to perform that task well are the only things great performers are concerned with.

CHAPTER 5 - SELF-IMAGE OF A WINNER

Having the Self-Image of a winner means that you possess the habits and attitudes of someone who believes that he or she is capable, competent, and willing to be successful. It means that you have the confidence that others lack while not being overly confident in your abilities. It means that you see yourself as one who has the necessary skills and the ability to reach your goals. It means that you are not afraid to think about success, talk about success, write about success, and goal set for the things you want to achieve in your life.

You can have passion, opportunity, train with purpose and discipline and be mentally strong under pressure, but if you do not build the Self-Image of a winner you will ultimately fall short of your true capabilities. Over the years I have seen hundreds of individuals that have the talent and tools to be successful, but for some reason they lack the belief that they can be great. There are many reasons why people fail to have the Self-Image needed in order to

ELEMENT #10

Elite Performers actively build and protect their Self-Image. Others fail to realize the importance of building and protecting their Self-Image.

reach the goals they want to achieve. The main reason is that most people do not know how to build the Self-Image needed to match the goals of the person they want to be.

The Self-Image of a person is how that individual sees him or herself to be. By thinking that you are not very good at something, even if you have great skill in that area, will force failure. You need to believe in yourself in order to be successful. This is why individuals who are less skilled than others can beat those who are more skilled. Skill helps, but without confidence and the belief that you can reach your goals you will never be able to take full advantage of your abilities.

Elite Performers actively build and protect their Self-Image. Others fail to realize the importance of building and protecting their Self-Image.

Before a person can build and protect the Self-Image they need, he or she, first needs to understand how Self-Image is built. It is not by accident that someone becomes great at what they do. It takes years of practice and thousands of positive imprints of doing things well to produce top performances. The Self-Image of an individual is the sum total of the imprints that one has over his or her career. If you take a beginner, he will have a small Subconscious Mind and a small Self-Image because he does not yet possess the necessary skill to do his task well, nor does he have the belief that he can achieve good results. The attitude of a beginner is one that wants to accomplish great things but is not yet programmed to do so.

Through practice and proper training you can build good subconscious skill while building a Self-Image of someone who is good. This Self-Image cannot grow without positive imprints from the Conscious Mind and Subconscious Mind. You must think appropriately. If you focus on the negative results, you will prohibit your Self-Image from growing and slow down your development in whatever area you are working. If you focus on your successes you will improve the growth of the Self-Image and therefore improve the probability for repeated success.

Every time you think about something it produces an imprint that is filed in the Self-Image. The Self-Image has one main job: to keep you where it believes you are. This is why the Conscious Mind plays a very important role in the imprinting process. How you respond or react to a task will magnify the imprints into the Self-Image. These imprints consist of the thoughts and actions of the individual. Every time you perform a task with a good result, your Self-Image will grow, and every time you perform a task with a bad result, your Self-Image will shrink.

Top performers not only focus on improving their subconscious ability, but they focus on building a Self-Image that matches their ability. This can only be done by being mentally disciplined in controlling what you think about before, during, and after an action. The best of the best are very good at thinking in a way that produces positive imprints into the Self-Image. This means that you must have a clear and defined way of thinking before and after a task.

If you do not have a clear and defined way of thinking you will allow the environment to take control of your thoughts. This is very evident in golf. For example, Tom and Tim are equal in physical and technical ability. Tom's thinking during play is a direct result of how he's playing. When Tom is playing well, his attitude is good. When Tom is playing poorly, his attitude is bad. The attitude and thought process that Tom has is based on what the environment is yielding. Tim, on the other hand, has a specific thought process before and after each shot. His attitude is not based on how he is playing. Tim focuses on his mental process and not on his results.

At a major tournament Tom and Tim are playing well. On hole fourteen things start to change. At the pace that Tom and Tim are playing, they will each finish strong and be close to a personal best. Coming down the stretch, Tom is set to play first and he immediately focuses on the water to the right side of the fairway. His first thought is, "Don't hit it right." This thought causes an imprint into the Self-Image. When Tom has a poor shot, it usually goes to the right. There are two possibilities that Tom has improved the likelihood of happening. The first is that he will hit it in the water. The second is that he will overcompensate and hit too far left. Both results are bad. As luck would have it, Tom hits it to the right and into the water. His reaction is a negative and quick one, "I suck! I can't believe this! I cost myself a good round. Way to go Tom!" This thought process becomes very emotional and keeps Tom from being able to play at his subconscious ability. The result is a

ELEMENT #11

Elite Performers reinforce success or focus on the correction. Others focus on the results and lack of success.

poor finish.

Tim has a different experience. He notices the water to the right, but instead of focusing on not hitting it to the right, he does what he has done all day. He first looks at where he wants to hit the shot and thinks about the execution of that particular shot. He runs a pre-planned mental program and gets set to play. His shot is to the left and in the rough. Although it is not a good result, Tim doesn't get angry. Unlike Tom, Tim thinks to himself, "How would I like to hit that shot over?" This thought process allows him the ability to play at his subconscious ability and achieve a good score. The key difference between these two performers is the way they think about themselves and the outcomes they are having. One is based on results; the other is based on process. Both thought processes feed imprints into the Self Image. Tom's approach only builds his Self-Image when he is playing well. Tim's approach builds his Self-Image when he is playing well and protects his Self-Image when he is playing poorly.

Elite Performers reinforce success or focus on the correction. Others focus on the results and lack of success.

There are three phases of a task. First, the anticipation phase represents the thought process and physical preparation of a task. Second, the action phase represents the time when the task is being performed. Third, the reinforcement phase represents the thought process of what you think about immediately after the task. All good performers know that you must have a good way of preparing for a task if you want a positive result. What separates the top performers from the rest is that top performers understand that you must focus on the right thing immediately after the task in order to consistently have good results. Having this thought process after the task will determine how successful you will be in the long run.

By focusing on your successes you will improve the probability of being more successful in the future. If you perform a task well, you should feast on that performance. The Self-Image needs self-praise in order to grow. Many performers have a misconception that they should always perform well and they do not give themselves credit when credit is warranted. If a baseball pitcher throws a perfect strike, he should think to himself, "That was a good pitch, and that's how you do it." This thought process should be a habit, because every time you give yourself credit when you perform well your Self-Image grows.

The imprints you have immediately after a task are critical to the growth of your Self-Image. If you never give yourself credit, how do you expect to gain any confidence for future performances? At the same time, if you do not have a good performance, beating yourself up will only slow down your opportunities for success.

If you are a very competitive person, odds are you will be hard on yourself and you will expect to reach your top level of ability when performing. How you handle the reinforcement phase will either increase the consistency of your performance or decrease the chances you have of winning. Not giving praise to yourself when performing well is one thing, but if you don't have a preplanned thought process after a task when the performance is bad it can lead to disaster. We will not always perform at our best, so how we handle any performance is critical to the Self Image.

Reinforcement of a task.

Top performers protect their Self-Image by having a planned thought process after performing a specific task. This process has three steps to it and is referred to as reloading. The purpose of reloading is to refresh the brain with the thought process of what you want while not getting caught up in what just happened. Successful people do not become engulfed in poor performances; they only focus on what they should do and not on what happened.

In 1987, I competed in my first World Championships, and I had the privilege of meeting a man named Malcom Cooper. My father had always spoken highly of Malcom and still has many great stories to share about him today. Malcom was the best rifle shooter in the 1980s. Many competitors feared him because he would shoot high scores consistently. His main accomplishment in sport was becoming the only person to ever win back-to-back Olympics in rifle shooting. I asked him what advantages he had over everyone else. After a long discussion it boiled down to one simple thing, he didn't think the same way the average shooter did.

He told me that he constantly focused on having a small

and slow hold before each and every shot. His thoughts were only on one thing, and it made sense. If you are only focusing on one thing, keeping the hold slow and small, it helps make the execution of the shot automatic. Most shooters try to shoot a good shot. Malcom was only trying to focus on having a slow and small hold and trusting that he would shoot a good shot. This may have given him some advantage over his competition, but most good shooters have a consistent thought process before the task. What gave Malcom his real advantage was his thought process after the task.

Malcom told me that the one thing I should listen to my dad about was the importance of controlling your thoughts after each shot. He was referring to the reinforcement phase. You must have a plan on what your thought process will be or you will fall victim to what the environment provides. If you have a plan that yields the best opportunity to help grow the Self Image you want, why would you ever think in a way that would prevent this from happening?

The point that Malcom was making is the most important piece of mental advice anyone can provide. What you allow yourself to think about after a task matters. These thoughts in the reinforcement phase can provide the necessary imprints into the Self-Image that will help ensure a strong Self-Image for future success.

When performing a task you must reload appropriately. If you beat yourself up over a poor performance you will increase the liklihood of having future poor performances. In order to increase the chances of having good performances in the future we must reinforce the correct thoughts. This thoughts process is referred to as reloading.

The reloading process begins immediately after the action and consists of three steps. These steps help organize the focus we need to have in order to build and protect the Self-Image we need. The first step is to evaluate your performance. When I am competing in rifle shooting, this step allows me to evaluate my previous shot. When evaluating the shot, I must put it into one of three categories. These categories are important because it helps to generate the correct imprint into the Self-Image. The first category is Great. If I shot a perfect shot, I would say "Great!" If the shot was not a perfect shot, but was still good, it would go into the second category, which is titled, "OK." An Ok shot is not great and not bad but somewhere in the middle.

When the shot is not Great or OK, it requires a special category. This category is worded in a specific way to ensure that the thought process is not a negative one. This thought process must also lead you into the second step. When a bad result occurs it must be put into the "Needs Work" category. The "Needs Work" category is the most important one, because it helps dilute any negative imprinting from the poor result achieved.

What do you picture when you hear yourself say "needs work?" You start to picture the correction of what needs improvement. This wording improves the probability of rehearsing the correction that needs to be made, while at the same time reducing any chances of dwelling on the bad result. Again, this is all about protecting the Self-Image.

If you focus on what needs work you automatically move into the second step of the reload, which is to rehearse the correction.

Rehearsing the correction helps bring closure to a result. If your performance was OK or needs work, you want to follow it up with an imprint of how you could make it better. The more vivid the imprint in the correction, the better closure you will have with the task. This is the best way you can improve and protect the Self-Image you need in order to reach the success you desire.

The final step of the reload is to let it go! Too many people hold on to things that they cannot control or do anything about. If you performed a bad shot or task, thinking about it and getting upset will not make the shot better. When this type of reaction occurs it only increases the chances of having more poor performances. You must move onto the next task at hand. The only way you can put yourself in the best position to do well is to bring closure to your current task, forget about it, and move onto your next one. This takes mental discipline and it's the best way you can achieve an advantage over your competition.

I tried to run the reloading process frequently in competitions. The days I ran this thought process I had my best performances and results. If I shot an okay shot I would say to myself, "OK," and picture what a better shot would look and feel like. I would immediately let it go and move onto the next shot. There is no time to count score, no time to compare yourself to others, no time to look at the leader board, and no time to feel sorry for yourself. The only thing that matters is to be disciplined in your thought process.

Think about the task you are performing and how you can implement the reinforcement phase into your task. This thought process is a mental tool that helps an individual focus on what is important. It is often the response you choose to your environment that determines your success. If you are focusing on what you should do, you cannot think about a negative result at the same time. If the outcome is positive, you should think about duplicating that performance and imprinting that thought before you let it go and move on. If you can do this, you will increase your performance, improve your results, and be more consistent under pressure.

Elite Performers focus on Attainment.
Others focus on Accomplishment.

Accomplishment is easy to measure. In school, accomplishment is measured by your grades; A, B, C, etc. In sports it's based on what place you finish; first, second, or third. In business it could be based on title, Vice President or CEO, or it could be based on how much money someone earns compared to another. No matter which example we look at, accomplishment compares our performance to others. Most performers focus on this measurement. Accomplishment is important, but it is not the sole focus of successful people.

When studying elite performers, we see that they use

ELEMENT #12
*Elite Performers focus on Attainment.
Others focus on Accomplishment.*

accomplishments to push themselves further and goal set for future performances, but they only use it as part of their focus. Attainment is their main goal, and it goes far beyond accomplishment.

Attainment is not easy to define. There are three ways to describe attainment. All three are important to the elite performer. The first part relates to accomplishment. Accomplishment is important because it is what causes someone to strive to push himself to do great things. When accomplishment becomes the sole focus, one's ability to reach his true potential is hindered. The next two parts of attainment are the defining factors in what separates a top performers ability to build his Self-Image from the Self-Image of his average competitor.

Self-Image is never built solely on accomplishments. Certainly, accomplishment aids in imprinting power to the Self-Image, but in order to reach high levels of achievement you must add the other two parts of attainment to determine your growth as a performer.

The second part of attainment relates to an ability that has been acquired through training. This ability enables the top performer to stay focused during training. You have to push yourself to new levels of ability in order to reach higher levels of accomplishment. This cannot be done if we only focus on results. We must focus on progress.

Focus on progress, not only on results.

An athlete will not gain the results he needs before he

obtains the necessary skills to reach a high level of accomplishment if results are his only goal. He must be able to perform at a high level under pressure and be consistent throughout his performance. This will not happen until he or she has built a base. A base is the foundation of skill that is mastered at a level that allows the individual the ability to take breaks and come back and perform at a high level. The athlete must master the basic skills needed to perform the tasks at hand well before he or she can build a base. Once the basics are mastered one can acquire advanced skills. Focusing on progress and not results is the fastest way to reach high levels of success.

When working with young athletes I focus on the overall progress they are making. Generally, I am not concerned with their score or how they finish in practice. I am only concerned about the amount of progress they are making in mastering the skill needed in order to be competitive. If I allow them to focus on their results and not concentrate on the progress that is being made it will slow down their growth in that sport.

The third part of attainment is the arrival at a new stage. We must strive to reach higher stages of learning if we expect to reach higher levels of success. The second and third parts of attainment should remain the focus of the person who wants to reach top level of success. If you are not pushing yourself to become great at what you do, it will make little difference in how great your skill level actually is. You must have both. Attainment is both becoming and accomplishing.

Becoming successful rarely happens by only accomplishing your goal. You can accomplish a goal but not experience the becoming part of attainment. When this happens it is unlikely that the experience can be duplicated. To prove this point, let's take a look at two individuals who have a goal of earning a million dollars. The first individual is a businessman who has been in business for years but has not yet reached the profit of a million dollars. He learned from his mistakes year to year until he finally reached his goal of earning a million dollars, reaching his goal. The second person bought a lottery ticket every week last year and on the second week of November he won the million-dollar lottery. Both men accomplished the same goal, but only one became something in the process.

The businessman has the ability to go out and duplicate his goal. He can use the same plan during his next year and expect to be able to reach the same profit. The second individual cannot rely on the same plan to achieve the same result. What is the possibility of him winning the lottery again, let alone each year being able to win more and more? The first individual who reached attainment is now in a position to set higher goals and achieve greater success. The difference of attainment verses accomplishment can be the difference between becoming a top performer or one who falls short of reaching his desired success.

If you want to reach the top level of your ability, you must focus on attainment. Becoming great at what you do doesn't stop at learning your craft. Attainment means mastering your craft, being able to focus consistently in pressure situations, having the confidence that you can succeed, and setting and reaching your goals. If you focus on the success points, build on your ability and incorporate these strategies in your plan, success becomes probable, not just possible.

THE 12 ELEMENTS

ELEMENT #1
Elite Performers are Passionate about what they do. Others like what they do.

Passion is the driving force that will move an individual with tens times the motivation to do what they need in order to succeed. If you are passionate about what you do, you are one step closer to success.

ELEMENT #2
Elite Performers manage their time and stick to a schedule. Others mismanage their time and don't have a schedule.

Time management is a necessary skill for success. Without proper time management, success will pass you by and find the person who is looking for it. Successful people control their time instead of allowing time to control their schedule.

ELEMENT #3

Elite Performers focus on opportunities. Others focus on obstacles.

Successful people view obstacles as learning opportunities they must go through in order to reach their goals. Opportunities are both created and looked for with the focus on taking advantage of the situation at hand.

ELEMENT #4

Elite Performers work on all three areas of performance. Others focus only on their subconscious ability.

In order to reach the highest level of success, one must focus on concentration, ability, and the confidence needed to obtain that success. It is not good enough just to be good in what you do. You must be good in all areas of performance.

ELEMENT #5

Elite Performers train with a purpose. Others practice what they enjoy.

Elite performers train with specific objectives. Purposeful practice is focusing and training on the areas of skill one needs to be mastered. If a skill is not mastered the performance will fall short.

ELEMENT #6
Elite Performers focus on Solutions.
Others focus on problems.

Solutions are the keys to success; problems are the locks that keep us out. By focusing on finding solutions you are one-step closure to finding the key to unlock the problem you are faced with.

ELEMENT #7
Elite Performers focus on what they should do.
Others focus on what happened.

It is not important what happened to you. What is most important is your focus on what you should do about what happened to you. Focusing on poor performance only creates the opportunity for more poor performances. Focus on the correction or feast on your success.

ELEMENT #8
Elite Performers focus on the process.
Others focus on outcome.

Process is primary. To gain the desired results you want, you must focus only on the process needed to achieve it.

Focusing on the outcome before the results occur is the distraction that top performers avoid. Elite performers are process oriented.

ELEMENT #9

Elite Performers give just the right amount of effort. Others try to give it 110 percent.

Giving it 110 percent is a guarantee that you will over try. To be the best means to give the right amount of effort needed in order to generate the best result possible.

ELEMENT #10

Elite Performers actively build and protect their Self-Image. Others fail to realize the importance of building and protecting their Self-Image.

In order to reach the highest level of ability, one needs to believe that they are capable of reaching that level. Self-belief and the confidence of your ability build the necessary Self-Image needed in order to be a winner.

ELEMENT #11

Elite Performers reinforce success or focus on the correction. Others focus on the result and lack of success.

Success comes by reinforcing the successes you have.

Elite performers do not dwell on their mistakes and failures. They view failure as an opportunity to learn, not as a way that they lost.

ELEMENT #12
Elite Performers focus on Attainment.
Others focus on Accomplishment.

In order to reach the level of accomplishment you desire, you first need to become the person who can obtain it. Becoming and accomplishing together provides the ability to reach the highest achievement level possible.

Contact Troy at:

Mental Management® Systems LLC
700 Parker Square
Suite 140
Flower Mound, TX 75028
ph. 972-899-9640
info@mentalmanagement.com
www.mentalmanagement.com

ABOUT THE AUTHOR

Troy Bassham is a Senior Master Instructor and Director of Systems Development at Mental Management® Systems LLC. Troy has been teaching Mental Management® since 1995. His main focus is helping players develop mental consistency during play, perform under pressure, build Self-Image of a winner, and training principles that focus on developing the mind and body at the same time. Troy's clients have won local, state, national and world events using Mental Management®. Troy has worked with hundreds of junior athletes with their mental game developing dozens of National Champions.

Troy used Mental Management® himself to win 12 National Championships in international rifle shooting, set 4 National Records and became the CISM World Champion.

Troy provides one on one, small group and large group training options.